First World War
and Army of Occupation
War Diary
France, Belgium and Germany

61 DIVISION
184 Infantry Brigade,
Brigade Trench Mortar Battery
5 July 1916 - 31 August 1916

WO95/3067/3

The Naval & Military Press Ltd
www.nmarchive.com
Published in association with The National Archives

Published by

The Naval & Military Press Ltd

Unit 10 Ridgewood Industrial Park,

Uckfield, East Sussex,

TN22 5QE England

Tel: +44 (0) 1825 749494

www.naval-military-press.com

www.nmarchive.com

This diary has been reprinted in facsimile from the original. Any imperfections are inevitably reproduced and the quality may fall short of modern type and cartographic standards.

© **Crown Copyright**
Images reproduced by permission of The National Archives, London, England, 2015.

Contents

Document type	Place/Title	Date From	Date To
Heading	WO95/3067/3		
War Diary	61st Division 184th Infy Bde Lt Trench Mortar Bty July-Aug 1916		
Heading	War Diary Of The 184th Light Trench Mortar Battery July 1st 1916 To July 31st 1916 Volume 3		
War Diary	La Gorgue	05/07/1916	06/07/1916
War Diary	Richebourg	07/07/1916	13/07/1916
War Diary	Laveutie	15/07/1916	15/07/1916
War Diary	Fauquissart	16/07/1916	23/07/1916
War Diary	Moated Grange	24/07/1916	31/07/1916
Heading	184 L. T. M. B. War Diary & Appendix Volume IV August 1916		
War Diary		01/08/1916	31/08/1916
Miscellaneous	184th Infantry Brigade Order No 23	30/07/1916	30/07/1916
Miscellaneous	Issued With 184th Inf Brigade Order No. 23		
Operation(al) Order(s)	184th Infantry Brigade Order No 24	08/08/1916	08/08/1916
Miscellaneous	Table B		
Miscellaneous	Table A		
Miscellaneous	Table C		
Miscellaneous	184 L I M B	14/08/1916	14/08/1916
Miscellaneous	A Form. Messages And Signals.		
Miscellaneous	Programme For Night 15/16 August 1916	15/08/1916	15/08/1916
Miscellaneous	A Form. Messages And Signals.		
Miscellaneous	The following programme will be carried out tonight 16/17 August Operation.	16/08/1916	16/08/1916
Miscellaneous	Reference G.243 para 7 for 9.30 rest 11.	17/08/1916	17/08/1916
Miscellaneous	The following programme will be carried out tonight 18/19 August Operation.	18/08/1916	18/08/1916
Operation(al) Order(s)	184th Brigade Order No 28	17/08/1916	17/08/1916
Miscellaneous	Amended Time Table "A" Issued with 164th Infantry Brigade Order No. 26.		
Miscellaneous	Artillery, H.T.M. L.T.M. & M.G. Programme for August 23rd.	22/08/1916	22/08/1916

3045/3067/3

61ST DIVISION
184TH INFY BDE

LT TRENCH MORTAR BTY
JLY - AUG 1916

SECRET   Vol III

WAR DIARY

of the

184th Light Trench Mortar Battery.

from July 1st 1916 to July 31st 1916

VOLUME 3.

WAR DIARY

INTELLIGENCE SUMMARY

(Erase heading not required.)

Army Form C. 2118.

Instructions regarding War Diaries and Intelligence Summaries are contained in F. S. Regs., Part II. and the Staff Manual respectively. Title pages will be prepared in manuscript.

Place	Date	Hour	Summary of Events and Information	Remarks and references to Appendices
La Gorgue	5-7-16	9 am	Physical Drill (½ hr)	2/Lt Ollard
"	"	10 am	Cleaning and inspecting guns (2 hrs)	2/Lt Byworth
"	"	2 pm	Gun Drill (1½ hrs)	2/Lt Byworth
"	"		Battery	2/Lt Ollard
6-7-16	"	8 am		
"	"	10 am	Route March via Estaires & Pont Riqueul, returned to billet 12.15 am	2/Lt Byworth
"	"	2.30pm	Gun & gun drill	2/Lt Ollard
"	"	5.20pm	Received orders to report to O.C. Batt. of B.H.Q. immediately, was ordered to proceed with Battery to S.8.A.9.2.5. a Centre of Transport. On being provided the Transport by supply Company were ranked on hay. 2/Lt Byworth, Sgt Lewin, looking party 3 men left La Gorgue 5.20pm	"
			2/Lt Ollard marched remainder of Battery with hand carts. Relief completed (118 NB) (BN2)	
			to 11.55 & reported to B.D.G. H.Q. Distributions as follows.	
			1 gun and Team S.4.B.9.2.	
			2 guns and Teams S.10.A.9.2.4	
			" " " S.10.C.1.2.5.	
			2/Lt Byworth T.M.B Officers Dugout S.10.C.2.4.	

Army Form C. 2118.

WAR DIARY
or
INTELLIGENCE SUMMARY
(Erase heading not required.)

Instructions regarding War Diaries and Intelligence Summaries are contained in F.S. Regs., Part II. and the Staff Manual respectively. Title pages will be prepared in manuscript.

Place	Date	Hour	Summary of Events and Information	Remarks and references to Appendices
Pickeburg	7.7.16	7 am	1 gun (L. ½ B&D front) S.4.B.9.2. remained in reserve. 4 guns (R.½ B&D front) were placed as follows: No. I S.10.c.3½.1. No. II S.10.c.7½.3. No. III S.10.d.0.5½. No. IV S.10.d.1.6.	J.E. Mueller
"	8.7.16	11am-11am	No. I gun fired 8 rounds enemy front line S.16.a.4.2.6. No. II " 7 " " " S.10.c.9.2. No. III " 7 " " " S.10.c.9.2. It was observed that enemy were using something which appeared with rods like two [sketch]	J.E. Mueller
"	9.7.16	4pm-2am	No. II gun fired 9 rounds enemy wire S.10.c.9.2. Gun emplacements commenced at S.10.d.3.2.½.	J.E. Mueller
"	10.7.16	12.30 pm	No. I gun fired 3 rounds at enemy wire S.10.c.9.1. but distance was too short to effect then engaged building emplacement S.10.66½	J.E. Mueller
"	11.7.16	6 pm	No. I gun fired 9 rounds at Bear Head, enemy direct hits. No. III gun fired 12 rounds at enemy front line S.10.2.0.3 - good results. One new emplacement completed and another one commenced during day and continued at night	J.E. Mueller
"	12.7.16	3 pm	Gun at S.10.d.3.2.1 (No.V) fired 9 rounds at Bear Head, several direct hits. " " S.10.6.9½ (No.II) signature on Sap A.2. " " S.10.d.0.5½ (No.III) .... emplacements completed	J.E. Mueller

WAR DIARY or INTELLIGENCE SUMMARY

Army Form C. 2118.

Place	Date	Hour	Summary of Events and Information	Remarks and references to Appendices
Bethune	13.7.16	11.7 pm	In support of raiding party - rapid fire from a line of 15 in 5" in 10 = 2 rounds per minute.	
		12 midnight	No I at S 16 a 2½.½ target S 16 c 7½.9	
			II " S.10 c 7.3½ " S 16 b 1½ 9¾	
			III " S 10 c 4 9¼ " S 10 d 2.2	
			IV " S 10 c 4.8 " S 10 d 3½ 2 } 487 rounds in all	
			V " S.10.c 6.9½ " S 10 a 8.5	
			VI " S.10 d 6¼ 9½ " S 11 c 9¾ 1	
Bethune	14.7.16		Relieved by 113 L.T.M.B. + proceeded to Le Hints marais.	J.C. Miller
Lawenti	15.7.16		Proceeded to billets at Rue de la Lys, Lawenti	J.C. Miller
Laugiesart	16.7.16	10 am	Guns in JOCKS LODGE. Preparing emplacement opposite Sugar Loaf.	J.C. Miller
"	17.7.16		" " " " "	J.C. Miller
"	18.7.16		Conveying & detonating 480 rounds and placing in frontline trench. Guns reported on Sugar Loaf.	J.C. Miller
"	19.7.16		Five guns in line - Bursting on Sugar Loaf - 4.30 pm. 30 rounds. 4 Guns ready to go over with assaulting infantry - two guns under 2/Lt Agworth later on. 2/Lt Bywater wounded. Guns brought back minus base plates. 7 R.C. bombers wounded during bombardment. Guns withdrawn at 10.30 pm. 10 casualties	J.C. Miller

Army Form C. 2118.

WAR DIARY
or
INTELLIGENCE SUMMARY.
(Erase heading not required.)

Instructions regarding War Diaries and Intelligence Summaries are contained in F.S. Regs., Part II. and the Staff Manual respectively. Title pages will be prepared in manuscript.

Place	Date	Hour	Summary of Events and Information	Remarks and references to Appendices
Laventie	20.7.16	9.30 am	Two guns in Flank Post. Two guns in Jocks Lodge. in reserve	J.C.Miller
"	21.7.16		"	J.C.Miller
"	22.7.16	10.30am	Guns withdrawn to billets. Ammunition collected into dumps in front line & FLANK POST. (400 rounds) Reorganization of gun teams	J.C.Miller
"	23.7.16	12. noon	Proceeded to billets in Rue Paradis, Laventie. Took over modern Lewis Gun Lectr from 1/8 S.T.M B	J.C.Miller
Moated Grange	24.7.16	10.30am	Four guns in GRANTS POST. Repair work to emplacements in front line.	J.C.Miller
"	25.7.16	7. am	N° I - M 24. c. 8. 2. registered on M 24. d. 4 ½. N° II M 30 a 2.15. M 30 a 3½ 4.	
			N° III M 30 a. 4. 1. " 30 a. 4. 1 IV M 36 d 9. 9 M 30 c 5. 1	
"		6.45pm	N° II 8 rounds on M 30 a. 5.5 (crater & barren)	J.C.Miller
"	26.7.16	11.30 am	N° II 12 rounds in retaliation for grenade fire	
		12.15 pm	N° II 5 " " " "	
		5.30 pm	N° I 2 " " " "	
		6.45 pm	N° III 15 " on M.G. emplacement - Fainer @ M 30 a. 5. 4. partial screen	
		9 pm	" 8 " " " " screen after changing position	J.C.Miller
		10.15 pm	N° IV 3 " in front line	
"	26.7.16	12.30 pm	N° II 3 " in retaliation for rifle grenade fire	J.C.Miller
		2.30 pm	N° I 5 " " " "	

Army Form C. 2118.

WAR DIARY
or
INTELLIGENCE SUMMARY.
(Erase heading not required.)

Instructions regarding War Diaries and Intelligence Summaries are contained in F.S. Regs., Part II. and the Staff Manual respectively. Title pages will be prepared in manuscript.

Place	Date	Hour	Summary of Events and Information	Remarks and references to Appendices
Noeux Grange Lorgue	26.7.16	4 pm	No IV - 4 rounds on enemy front line where working party was observed	
		6 pm	No I - registered on craters M 30 a 6.5 & 5.6	
		8.30 pm	No I - 20 rounds (traversing) - Craters M 30 a 6.8 and 5.6 where patrols were reported	
		"	No IV - 6 " - enemy front line trench	
		"	No IV - 10 " - " "	
		"	No IV - 5 " - " "	
	27.7.16	11.30 am	No I - 5 " - in reply to rifle grenade fire	
		2.30 pm	Gun teams relieved. Destroyed emplacement rebuilt.	J.R. Miller
		8.30 pm	No I - 10 rounds - point M 22 d 6½ - 3	
		"	No I - 8 " - enemy wire where gap is reported	
		"	No IV - 10 " - do do	
		"	No IV - 12 " - do do	
	28.7.16	4.30 pm	No I - 30 " - on enemy trench running from M 30 a 5.3. & M 30 a 6.5	
		"	No IV - 30 " - do do	
		"	No IV - 15 " - on M 24 d 6½ & 3	
		"	No IV - 15 " - on M 30 c 5.5.	J.R. Miller

Army Form C. 2118.

WAR DIARY
or
INTELLIGENCE SUMMARY.
(Erase heading not required.)

Instructions regarding War Diaries and Intelligence Summaries are contained in F. S. Regs., Part II. and the Staff Manual respectively. Title pages will be prepared in manuscript.

Place	Date	Hour	Summary of Events and Information	Remarks and references to Appendices
Inskr Gorge	28.7.16	8.45 p.m	No I & III opened fire on enemy trench manning M30 a 41. 5 M 30 a 5½ 3 — 20 rounds	J.F.R. Miller
	29.7.16	11.30 am	No II fired on enemy front line — 5 rounds	
		6.45 pm	No I fired on crater M 30 a 6.8 — 15 rounds	J.R. Miller
		"	III " M30 a 56 — 10 "	
	30.7.16	6.45 pm	No II replied with 5 rounds to enemy minenwerfer	
		9.0 pm	No I fired on crater M30 a 6.6½ — 6 rounds	J.F.R. Miller
		"	No II " fired " M 30 a 5½ 4½ — 5 rounds	J.F.R. Miller
		"	No IV " " M30 a 5.11½ — 5 rounds	
	31.7.16	6.0 pm	No II & No III fired 10 rounds each in cooperation with M.T.M's on C.T. front line M30 a 5½ 2½	

J.F.R. Miller St Capt Comdg
1st Right Trench Mortar Battery

Confidential

184 L.T.M.B.

WAR DIARY & APPENDIX

VOLUME IV
AUGUST
1916

Army Form C. 2118.

WAR DIARY
or
INTELLIGENCE SUMMARY.
(Erase heading not required.)

184 LIGHT TRENCH MORTAR BATTERY.

No. 1

Place	Date	Hour	Summary of Events and Information	Remarks and references to Appendices
	Aug 1st		Battery was relieved by 182nd T.M.B. & proceeded to billets at La Gorgue	Ref: app:- (1)
	Aug. 2nd to 8th inclusive		Reveille 5.30. General training; physical drill, gun drill, arms drill, route marches etc: from 6.0.A.M. till 8.0.A.M. & from 9.0.A.M. till 12.0 noon.	
	Aug. 9th		Battery relieved part of 182nd T.M.B. & 183rd T.M.B in the Tanquissart section.	Ref app:- (2)
	" "	6.30 PM 8.0 PM	Six Guns in front line were registered on enemy front line. 10 rounds were fired.	
	" "	8.30.P.M.	Guns occupied emplacements N.13.a.9½.3. — N.14.a.2.6. — N.13.b.2.6.	
	" 11th		Fire was opened at 1.0.A.M. (in conjunction with Artillery, M.T.M. & M.G.) on enemy front line. 161 rounds was fired.	
	" "	6.0.P.M.	Guns 9.0: 4. 6. & 12. registered on enemy front line at N.19.a.4.6. — N.13.C.9¾.3. — & N.14.a.9½.6¼.	
	" 12th		Much work was done in repairing & improving emplacements.	
	" 13th		Fire was opened at 3.30.A.M. (in conjunction with M.T.M. & M.G.) on enemy wire, lifting to enemy parapet at 3.45.A.M. from front N.19.a.3.5. to N.13.C.9.2. 88 rounds was fired.	
	" 14th		Work commenced on new battle emplacement (in conjunction with P.E.) at N.14.a.1½.4½.	
	14/15 Aug 15		Commencing at 12.0. midnight, fire was opened by 2 guns (in conjunction with Artillery & M.T.Ms) on enemy wire from N.13.d.9.6½. to N.14.a.5.0. 198 rounds were fired.	Refs app:- (3)

Army Form C. 2118.

184 LIGHT TRENCH MORTAR BATTERY.

No. .... (2.) ....
Date ....

WAR DIARY
or
INTELLIGENCE SUMMARY.
(Erase heading not required.)

Instructions regarding War Diaries and Intelligence Summaries are contained in F. S. Regs., Part II. and the Staff Manual respectively. Title pages will be prepared in manuscript.

Place	Date	Hour	Summary of Events and Information	Remarks and references to Appendices
Contd...	Aug 15		In conjunction with Artillery & M.T.M. & M.G. fire was opened at 10.0.P.M. on enemy's front line between N.13.c.5½.1 & N.13.d.1½.5. with good results.	Refs: Appen. (4.)
	" 16.		Rounds fired 114.	
	" 16.		During the day work was done on new trench emplacement & replenishing Ammunition Store.	
	Aug 17	2.0.a.m.	In connection with Artillery & M.T.M. 30 rounds were fired by gun at N.8.c.21; objective, enemy front line between N.14.a.9½.7. & N.14.a.6.3.	
	" 17.	2.30 a.m.	30 rounds were fired by gun at N.18.c.9½.1.; objective, enemy front line between N.19.a.6½.9 & N.19.a.4.5.	Refs: Appen. (5)
	" "	2.0 hrs	30 rounds were fired by gun at N.14.a.1.3.; objective, enemy front line between N.14.c.½.9 & N.14.c.2½.7. In each case rounds of fire were given, tried to explode together & good results were obtained.	
	" "	4.0.P.M.	Gun teams relieved.	
	" "	11.45 a.m.	Gun at N.14.a.1.2. registered on enemy front at N.14.a.5½.1½. & at 4.0.P.M. on N.14.c.3½.7.	Refs: Appen. (6)
	" "		7 rounds were fired	
	" "	11.35 P.M.	Gun at N.14.a.1.2 fired 50 rounds, traversing enemy front line from N.14.c.2½.½. & to N.14.c.5.9.	

Instructions regarding War Diaries and Intelligence Summaries are contained in F. S. Regs., Part II. and the Staff Manual respectively. Title pages will be prepared in manuscript.

WAR DIARY
or
INTELLIGENCE SUMMARY.
(Erase heading not required.)

194 LIGHT TRENCH MORTAR BATTERY. No. 3. Date

Army Form C. 2118.

Place	Date	Hour	Summary of Events and Information	Remarks and references to Appendices
	Aug: 18th	5.15 P.M.	No 11 Gun registered on N.14.c.4.8. firing 4 rounds with satisfactory results.	
	" "	11.10 to 11.20 P.M.	In conjunction with Artillery & M.T.M. No: 10 Gun opened fire on N.14.a.5¾.1 to N.14.c.2¼.7½ firing 40 rounds with graduated fuses.	Ref: append (7)
	" "	11.45 to 11.55 P.M.	No 3. Gun opened fire on M.24.d.8.4¾ to M.24.d.4.½. firing 40 rounds.	
	" 19	12.40 to 12.50 AM.	No 10 Gun opened fire on N.14.a.5¾.1 to N.14.c.2¼.7½. firing 20 rounds.	
	" 19th	10.40 P.M.	Guns at N.14.a.1½.2. N.14.a.1½.4. & N.14.a.1½.5. opened fire on N.14.c.3.7¼. N.14.c.4½.8¼. & N.14.a.6½.2½.	
	" "	10.42 P.M.	Guns lifted to Support Line for 3 min & then switched ~~from~~ to N.14.c.¼.6. to N.14.c.1¾.6¼. & N.14.a.6½.2½. 363 rounds were fired	Ref append (8)
	" "	10.40 P.M.	Gun at N.13.c.6.6½. fired 38 rounds on enemy front line drawing some retaliation.	
	" 20th	1.15 AM.	Guns at N.14.a.1½.2. & N.14.a.1½.5. again opened on N.14.c.3.7¼. & N.14.a.6½.2½. 93 rounds being fired.	
	" 20th	9.15 P.M.	In co-operation with Artillery Gun at N.13.c.2½.3. opened fire on N.13.c.8½.1. for 2 minutes then switched to N.19.a.6¾.9. for 13 minutes traversing fire. 87 rounds were fired.	
	" 21st		Much work was carried out during the day replenishing Ammunition store.	

Army Form C. 2118.

Instructions regarding War Diaries and Intelligence Summaries are contained in F. S. Regs., Part II. and the Staff Manual respectively. Title pages will be prepared in manuscript.

WAR DIARY
or
INTELLIGENCE SUMMARY.
(Erase heading not required.)

164 LIGHT TRENCH MORTAR BATTERY
No. 4
Date

Place	Date	Hour	Summary of Events and Information	Remarks and references to Appendices
	Aug 21st	5.40 A.M.	Gun at M. 24.c. 9½.8. opened fire on crater, firing 92 rounds. Results were satisfactory the explosions taking place on the near lip & inside crater. Retaliation was heavy with Minenwerfer & Torpedoes close to front & on support lines.	
			During the day work was done on new emplacements	
			Gun teams were relieved at 3.0.P.M.	
	Aug 22nd	2.15.P.M.	10 rounds were fired on N.19.a. 5¾.8. At 2.30.P.M. 10 rounds were fired on N.13.d.1.3½.	
	"	2.15.P.M.	12 " " " " N.13.c. 8½.1¼ " 3.0 P.M 10 " " " " N.14.c.3.7.	
	"	3.15 P.M.	10 " " " " N.13.c. 9¾.2¾ " 3.40.P.M. 15 " " " " N.19.a.4.6½.	
	"	4.0.P.M.	15 " " " " N.13.c. 8½.1¼ " 4.30.P.M 12 " " " " N.14.c. 2¼.6½	
	"	5.30.P.M.	10 " " " " N.19.a.8.9½ " 6.15.P.M. 20 " " " " N.13.c.10.1½.	
	"	7.0.P.M.	10 " " " " N.19.a. 6½.9½ " 7.30.P.M. 20 " " " " N.13.d.1.3½.	
			154 rounds were fired & result was satisfactory, duckboards & sandbags being thrown into the air at most of the points fired on.	
	Aug			

Army Form C. 2118.

124 LIGHT TRENCH MORTAR BATTERY

No. ....
Date 5

Instructions regarding War Diaries and Intelligence Summaries are contained in F. S. Regs., Part II. and the Staff Manual respectively. Title pages will be prepared in manuscript.

WAR DIARY
or
INTELLIGENCE SUMMARY.
(Erase heading not required.)

Place	Date	Hour	Summary of Events and Information	Remarks and references to Appendices
	Aug 23rd	11.48.A.M.	Gun at N.13.C.3½.4. fired on N.13.C.8½.1.	
		12.30 P.M.	" N.24.C.9.3. " Crater at M.24.d.2½.1.	
		1.30 P.M.	" N.14.a.1.5 " N.14.a.6.2.	
		3.0 P.M.	" N.14.a.1.2 " N.13.d.9½.6.	
		3.45 P.M.	" N.13.C.5.6½ " N.13.C.9¾.2¾.	
		4.30 P.M.	" N.14.a.1.5 " N.14.a.5¼.1.	
		5.30 P.M.	" N.13.C.3½.4 " N.13.C.10.1¼.	
		6.10 P.M.	" N.14.a.1.2. " N.14.C.1.6½.	
		6.50 P.M.	" N.13.C.5.6½ " N.13.C.8.1½.	
		7.20 P.M.	" N.14.a.1.5. " N.14.a.6½.2½.	
		9.30 P.M.	in conjunction with Artillery & M.T.M. fire was opened on Craters at M.24.D.2½.1. Refs. appear for 5 minutes & on Front Line & C.T.s after that time for a further 10 minutes.	(9)
			In all 216 rounds were fired.	
	Aug 24		Fire was opened at various times during the day on enemy Front Line & C.T.s. During the day a complete count was made of all Stokes Ammunition & Cartridges in the Front Line, & work was done in cleaning & improving emplacements.	

T2134. Wt. W708—776. 500000. 4/15. Sir J. C. & S.

Army Form C. 2118.

184 LIGHT TRENCH MORTAR BATTERY.

No. 6

Date ....

WAR DIARY
or
INTELLIGENCE SUMMARY.
(Erase heading not required.)

Instructions regarding War Diaries and Intelligence Summaries are contained in F. S. Regs., Part II. and the Staff Manual respectively. Title pages will be prepared in manuscript.

Place	Date	Hour	Summary of Events and Information	Remarks and references to Appendices
	Aug 25th	11.30.A.M.	Gun at N.8.c.3.1. registered on N.14.a.9½.6. (enemy wire)	
		12.0. NOON.	" " N.13.c.3½.4 fired on front line at N.13.c.8½.1.	
		2.30.P.M.	" " N.8.c.3.1 " " " " N.14.a.9½.6. &	
			" " M.18.d.8.0. " " wire at N.19.a.5½.8¼	
	4.0.P.M.		" " N.14.a.1.5. " " Red River & front line obtaining good results - Duckboards & corrugated iron being thrown into the air.	
	6.45.P.M.		Gun at N.8.c.3.1 opened on front line from N.14.a.9½.6. to N.14.a.9¾.7.	
			" " N.14.a.1.5. " " " " at N.14.a.6½.2½. but had to cease fire after 4 rounds owing to legs of gun bending.	
	7.0.P.M.		Gun at N.13.c.3½.4. opened on front line & wire from N.13.c.8½.1 to N.13.c.9½.2.	
			" " N.13.c.2½.3. also opened on front line at N.19.a.5½.8.	
	26th	4.45.A.M.	" " N.13.c.2½.3. fired on gap in wire at N.19.a.5½.8¼.	
			In all 203 rounds were fired, provoking rather heavy retaliation from the enemy, who replied with H.E on Rue Tilleloy & Support Lines, & Aerial Torpedoes on front line.	

T2134. Wt. W708—776. 500000. 4/15. Sir J. C. & S.

WAR DIARY or INTELLIGENCE SUMMARY

Army Form C. 2118.

184 LIGHT TRENCH MORTAR BATTERY

Place	Date	Hour	Summary of Events and Information	Remarks and references to Appendices
	Aug 26	2.30 P.M.	Gun at N.13.c.2½.3. fired 10 rounds on enemy front line in reply to rifle grenades & silenced them successfully.	
	" "	7.0 P.M.	Gun at M.18.d.8.0. opened fire on O.P. H.12 (M.19.a.5½.8) &	
			" N.14.a.1.2 " " Enemy wire at N.14.c.4.8½.) then both lifted on to enemy front line with good results. 45 rounds were fired.	
	" 27	4.0 A.M.	Gun at N.8.c.3.1. fired 25 rounds traversing fire on enemy front line & wire at N.14.a.9½.5½.	
	" "	5.15 A.M.	Gun at N.8.c.3.1. fired 48 rounds on enemy front line at N.14.a.9.5½. Enemy heavy retaliation with 5.9's & rifle grenades, which proved ineffective.	
	" "	8.30 AM to 11.0 A.M.	Enemy front line was bombarded by 4 guns between N.14.r.½.8 & N.13.c.9.6. in all 185 rounds were fired & good results were observed. Enemy retaliated at intervals with rifle grenades on front line & with 4.2s & 5.9s on Tilleloy & Pinacotin.	
	" "	7.0 P.M.	7 rounds were registered on N.13.c.8.2. Enemy replied with 4.2s on support lines.	
	" 28	8.0 A.M.	Gun at N.8.c.3.1. fired 50 rounds at head of enemy C.T. at N.14.a.9½.5½.	
	" "	11.0 A.M.	Gun at N.13.c.3½.4. opened on enemy front line between N.13.d.4.3½. & N.13.c.9½.1½. in reply to a few small aerial torpedoes.	

Army Form C. 2118.

184 LIGHT
TRENCH MORTAR
BATT——

No. 8
Date ....

WAR DIARY
or
INTELLIGENCE SUMMARY.
(Erase heading not required.)

Instructions regarding War Diaries and Intelligence Summaries are contained in F. S. Regs., Part II. and the Staff Manual respectively. Title pages will be prepared in manuscript.

Place	Date	Hour	Summary of Events and Information	Remarks and references to Appendices.
	Aug 28	4.0.P.M. to 4.45.P.M.	In conjunction with Artillery, enemy front line, wire & M.Gs were bombarded by Guns at N.14.a.1.2; N.14.a.1.5; & N.8.c.3.1. (with 3 guns on left Sub-section) & Guns at M.18.d.8.0. & N.13.c.3½.4. In all 505 rounds were fired.	
	" 29		At intervals during the day guns at M.18.d.8.0. & N.13.c.3½.3. replied to enemy rifle grenades & silenced them successfully.	
	" "	4.0.P.M.	Gun at N.8.c.3.1. opened on enemy front line at N.14.a.8½.6. & wire in front of this point, drawing light retaliation on Tilleloy.	
	" "	7.0.P.M.	Gun at N.13.c.3½.4. opened on enemy front line & wire about N.13.c.8½.1 with good results. In all 69 rounds were fired but owing to very bad weather & flooded emplacements firing was much interfered with.	
	" 30		During the day our guns promptly replied to & silenced enemy rifle grenades. There was very little activity in enemy lines. Difficulty was experienced in draining floors of emplacements & rendering base plates secure; further rain in the afternoon impeded our progress & rendered firing extremely difficult. Work was also done to render Ammunition store rainproof. During the day 26 rounds were fired.	

Army Form C. 2118.

184 LIGHT TRENCH MORTAR BATTERY.
No. 9
Date............

WAR DIARY
or
INTELLIGENCE SUMMARY.
(Erase heading not required.)

Instructions regarding War Diaries and Intelligence Summaries are contained in F. S. Regs., Part II. and the Staff Manual respectively. Title pages will be prepared in manuscript.

Place	Date	Hour	Summary of Events and Information	Remarks and references to Appendices
	Augt 31st	11.0.A.M.	Gun at 9704 emplacement registered on enemy front line.	
	" "	7.0 P.M.	An organised shoot took place on the right & left sub-sections on enemy front line & wire at N.19.a.5½.8 — N.19.a.3½.6 — N.14.a.6½.2½ — N.14.a.9½.6. 299 rounds were fired with very satisfactory results; enemy parapet & duckboards being destroyed; & at N.19.a.3½.6 the gap in the wire was widened. At N.14.a.9½.6. observer reported that a machine gun was thrown into the air. Retaliation was rather heavier than usual on our C.T.s & reserve line, with a lesser amount on our front line; a large proportion of the enemy shells were blind.	

A.J. Raymond Miller Capt
Commanding 184th L.T.M.B.

NOT TO BE TAKEN IN THE TRENCHES.   Copy No.

SECRET   30/7/16.

184TH INFANTRY BRIGADE ORDER NO. 23

Reference
Trench Maps,
BETHUNE Combined
and Sheet 36A.

1. The 184 Infantry Brigade will be relieved by the 182 Infantry Brigade on the 1st August- In accordance with Table A. attached.

2. Details of Relief to be arranged between Officers Commanding concerned.

3. LONELY STREET will not be used except for the purpose of relieving ERITH POST.

4. Reconnoitring Officers from 182 Infantry Brigade will report at Headquarters of Battalions holding the front line during the morning of the 31st inst.

5. Receipts for Trench Stores, Maps, Aeroplane Photographs and documents handed over to reach Brigade Headquarters by 9 a.m. 2nd inst.

6. Code for completion of relief :-

    "COME UP, I SAY COME UP".

7. A Staff Officer will be at Headquarters LA GORGUE from 3 p.m. Brigade Headquarters closes at COCKSHY HOUSE at 6 p.m. and opens at LA GORGUE at the same hour.

Issued at :- 7.30 p.m.

Received 9:25 PM.

                                            E.C. Capp.
                                            Major
                                            Brigade Major
                                            184th Infantry Brigade.

    Copy No. 1 to 5   Bde. Staff.
             6   4/Oxfords.
             7   4/Royal Berks.
             8   5/Glosters.
             9   2 Bucks.
            10   184 Machine Gun Coy.
            11   184 Light Trench Mortars.
            12   Right Group, R.F.A.
            13   No. 1. Coy. R.E.
            14   Pioneer Battalion.
            15   3 Fd. Amb.
            16   61 Div.
            17   No. 4. Coy. A.S.C.
            18   182 Inf. Bde.
            19   183 Inf. Bde.
            20   93 Inf. Bde.

ISSUED WITH 184TH INF BRIGADE ORDER NO.23.

TABLE A.

No.	Unit.	Relieved by.	Proceed to Billets at	Starting Point.	Time.	Route.	Remarks.
1.	5/Glosters.	5/Warwicks.	W. end of LA GORGUE	—	—	LE DRUMEZ–LA GORGUE	Relief to be completed by 6 p.m.
2.	4/R.Berks with 2 Coys. 2/Bucks attached.	7/Warwicks.	LA GORGUE SQUARE (2 Coys 2/Bucks to LE Gd PACAUT	—	—	Ditto.	Ditto.
3.	184 M.G.Coy.	182 M.G.Coy.	M.2.c.9.5.	—	—	Ditto.	Ditto.
X 4.	184 L.T.M.	182 L.T.M.	K.35.b.6.3.	—	—	—	
5.	2/Bucks Less 2 Coys.	8/Warwicks relieve POSTS.	LE Gd. PACAUT	—	8-30 a.m.	LE DRUMEZ–LA GORGUE–LE Gd–PACAUT	Relief of POSS to be completed by 12 noon.
6.	4/Oxfords.	6/Warwicks. 8/Warwicks.	ROBERMETZ	Road Junction H.12.c.6.8.	6.6.8.	PONT ROCHON–LA GORGUE–K.28.d.–ROBERMETZ.	

NOT TO BE TAKEN IN THE TRENCHES.   Copy No. 11.

SECRET

184TH INFANTRY BRIGADE ORDER NO. 24

August 8th, 1916.

Reference Maps
Sheets 36 & 36a
$\frac{1}{40000}$ Trench Maps.

(2)

1. On the 9th August, the Brigade will take over the FAUQUISSART Section, which will extend from M.24.c.6.1. to BOND ST inclusive.
    Reliefs in accordance with Table A attached.

2. On August 8th, the 2/BUCKS will move to Billets about L.34.b. reaching there at 6 p.m.

3. Brigade Boundaries are :-

    Northern - BOND ST inclusive - M.6.d.5.6. - just N. of LAVENTIE STATION.

    Southern - M.24.c.6.1. (SOUTH EASTERN RAILWAY exclusive) - LA FLINQUE Road exclusive - M.16.b.6.4.

4. Table B attached shows the POSTS etc to be held. Permanent garrisons will not be used for counter-attack unless ordered. Garrisons of Posts and supporting platoons may be used for work in the Front line.

5. Table C. attached shows disposition of Machine Gun Company.

6. Details of Reliefs will be arranged between O.C. Units concerned.

7. The reliefs of the Machine Gun Company and Light Trench Mortars will be completed by 12 noon.
    The relief of the Infantry Battalions by 6 p.m.

8. Completion of Reliefs to be reported to Brigade Headquarters.
    Code for completion :- " SEND UP 100 STEEL HELMETS".

9. List of Maps, Aeroplane Photographs, and Trench Stores taken over will be sent to Brigade Headquarters by 9 a.m. 10th August.
    A disposition return will be forwarded as soon as possible.

10. Brigade Headquarters closes at LA GORGUE at 4-30 p.m and opens at LAVENTIE, M.4.b.2.6. at the same hour.
    G.O.C. 184th Infantry Brigade assumes command of the FAUQUISSART Section as extended at 6 p.m.

ACKNOWLEDGE.

Issued at :- 3/pm

E.C. Capps
Major
Brigade Major
184th Infantry Brigade.

P.T.O.

NOTES ON TANKS IN THE TRENCHES.   Copy No.

184TH INFANTRY BRIGADE ORDER NO. 24

August 6th, 1916.

Reference Maps
TRENCH 36 & 36a
1
ADGOU
AREA.

1. On the 9th August, the Brigade will take over the FAUQUISSART Section, which will extend from N.Co.c.2.5 ....
Tanks A attached.

2. On August 9th .... will move to Billets about B.H.Q. res .... at 6 p.m.

3. Machine .... relieve M.G.A.S.C.
PRIVATE ADVANCE STATION.

Southern .... (SOUTH EASTERN RAILWAY) .... A TILMOUT Road exclusive

Copy No. 1. to 5. Bde Staff.
6. 4/Oxfords.
7. 4/Royal Berks.
8. 5/Glosters.
9. 2/Bucks.
10. 184 Machine Gun Company.
11. 184 Light Trench Mortars.
12. 2 Field Coy, R.E.
13. 3 Field Coy. R.E.
14. 183rd Infantry Brigade.
15. 182 Infantry Brigade.
16. No. 4. Coy. A.S.C.
17. 2 Field Amb.
18. 61 Div.
19. Left Group, R.F.A.

4. Tests .... shown the POSTS als to be held. PRESENT .... reinforce will not be used for counter-attack. GARRISONS .... Own and supporting platoons may be used for work on the front line.

5. Table C. attached shows disposition of Machine Gun Company.

6. Details of Reliefs will be arranged between O.C. Units concerned.

7. The reliefs of the Machine Gun Company and Light Trench Mortars will be completed by 12 noon.
The relief of the Infantry Battalions by 6 p.m.

8. Completion of Reliefs to be reported to Brigade Headquarters.
Code for completion :- " SEND UP 100 STEEL HELMETS".

9. List of Maps, Aeroplane Photographs, and Trench Stores taken over will be sent to Brigade Headquarters by 9 a.m. 10th August.
A disposition return will be forwarded as soon as possible.

10. Brigade Headquarters closes at LA ROUQUE at 5-30p.m. and opens at LAVENTIE, M.4.b.2.5. at the same hour.
O.C. 184th Infantry Brigade assumes command of the FAUQUISSART Section as extended .... at 6 p.m.

ACKNOWLEDGE.

Issued at:- 3pm
.... Major
Brigade Major
184th Infantry Brigade.

P.T.O.

ISSUED WITH 184TH INFANTRY BRIGADE ORDER NO.24.

TABLE "B".

POSTS.	Held by.	Strength.	Remarks.
ERITH POST	Right Front Battalion.	1 Platoon.	Permanent Garrison.
ELGIN POST	"	1 Platoon.	Permanent Garrison.
M.24.a.8.5.	"	1 Platoon.	Supporting Platoon.
FAUQUISSART	"	1 Platoon.	Permanent Garrison.
N.13.a.2.5.	"	1 Platoon.	Supporting Platoon.
N.13.b.9.8.	Left Front Battalion.	1 Platoon.	Supporting Platoon.
FLANK.	"	1 Platoon.	Permanent Garrison.
A.1.	"	1 Platoon.	Permanent Garrison.
LONELY	Right Reserve Battalion.	1 Platoon.	Move by night to positions in the Reserve Line and at disposal of O.C. Right Sub-Section for counter-attack.
ROAD BEND	"	1 Platoon.	
WANGERIE.	"	1 Platoon.	
MASSELOT.	"	1 Platoon.	
HOUGOUMONT	Left Reserve Battalion.	1 Platoon.	Move by night to positions in the Reserve line and at disposal of O.C. Left Sub-Section for Counter-attack.
DEAD END.	"	2 Platoons.	
PICANTIN.	"	1 Platoon.	

ISSUED WITH 184TH INFANTRY BRIGADE ORDER NO.24.

UNIT.	Taking over	Relieving	Starting Point	Time.	Remarks.
1. 2/Bucks with 1 Company 5/Glosters attached.	Front Line from (1) M.24.c.6.1. to ERITH ST incl. (2) ERITH ST excl. to N.13.c.8.7½.	7/Warwicks 182 Inf.Bde. 8/Worcesters. 183 Inf.Bde.			
2. 4/Oxfords.	Front Line from N.13.c.3.7½ to BOND ST exclusive.	4/Glosters.			East of Level crossing G.31.d., all movements will be by platoons – at 100 x distance.
3. 4/R.Berks.	Left Reserve Battn.	6/Glosters.	Road junction L.34.b.8.2.	8-15 a.m.	
4. 5/Glosters. less 1 Coy.	Right Reserve Battn.	7/Worcesters.	Road junction L.34.d.5.9.	8-45 a.m.	S. & E. of LAVENTIE by parties of not more than 10 men at 50 yards distance.
5. 184 Machine Gun Coy.		2 Guns 182 M.G.Coy. and 183 M.G.Coy.			
6. 184 Light Trench Mortars.		Part of 182 L.T.M's & 183 L.T.M's.			

ISSUED WITH 184TH INFANTRY BRIGADE ORDER NO. 24.

TABLE "C"

POSITION OF MACHINE GUNS.

POSITION.	MAP REFERENCE ETC.	NUMBER OF GUNS.
(a) FRONT LINE	M. 24. c.7.1.	1 GUN.
	M. 24. b.5.1.	1 GUN.
	N. 13.d.4.9½.	1 GUN.
	N. 14.a.2.3.	1 GUN.
	N. 8.d.1.8.	1 GUN.
(b) FRONT LINE POSTS.	FAUQUISSART POST	1 GUN.
	FLANK POST	1 GUN.
(c) 2ND LINE POSTS.	CINEMA HOUSE.	1 GUN.
	C.R.A's HOUSE.	1 GUN.
	MASSELOT HOUSE.	2 GUNS.
	COPSE.	1 GUN.
	JOCKS LODGE.	2 GUNS.
(d) IN RESERVE.		2 GUNS.

SECRET.

4 Oxfords.	2 Field Coy.
4 Royal Berks.	3 Field Coy.
5 Glosters.	"A" Coy Pioneers.
2 Bucks Bde	No 3 Aust Tunnelling Coy.
Bde Signal Officer.	61st Division.
Left Group R.F.A.	184 S.T.M.B.
15 Aust Bde.	
182 Inf Bde.	

---

1. The following programme will be carried out tonight 14/15 August.

    1. 0.00 - 0.10. Medium Trench Mortars (3 Mortars), Light Trench Mortars (2 Mortars) to concentrate on enemy's wire from N.13.d. 9.6½. to N.14.a.5.0. Rifle Grenades on front trench.

    2. 0.11. - 0.20. Concentrate on enemy's front trench.

    3. 0.21. - 0.25. Lift on to enemy's second line. (No Rifle Grenades

    4. 0.26. - 0.35. Same as 2.

    5. 0.36. - 0.40. Same as 3.

    6. 0.37½ - 0.40. Vickers traversing Front Line and Rifle Grenades on to front line.

2. Particular attention will be paid to enemy mine shafts.

3. The Artillery will co-operate in the above.

4. One Vickers will be in the neighbourhood of N.8.5. (arrangements be made with 15th Aust Bde), so as to enfilade the enemy's front line.

5. The Medium and Light Trench Mortars will fire 2 days ammunition per mortar.

6. Zero time will be 12 midnight.

7. Watches will synchronized by Bde Signal Officer at 8 p.m. by code on the telephone.

Acknowledge

August 14th 1916.

Major. Brigade Major.
184th Infantry Brigade.

"A" Form. Army Form C. 2121.
MESSAGES AND SIGNALS.

Prefix......Code......m.	Words	Charge	This message is on a/c of:	Recd. at......m.
Office of Origin and Service Instructions.	Sent		....................Service.	Date..............
	At..........m.			From.............
	To........		(Signature of "Franking Officer.")	By..............
	By........			

TO

| Sender's Number. | Day of Month. | In reply to Number. | A A A |
| G312 | 15 | | |

Acknowledge 15/8/16

From 1st Inf Bde
Place
Time 3.45pm

"A" Form.
MESSAGES AND SIGNALS.
Army Form C. 2121.

Prefix	Code	m.	Words	Charge	This message is on a/c of:	Recd. at	m.
Office of Origin and Service Instructions.			Sent		Service.	Date	
Priority			At	m.		From	
			To			By	
			By		(Signature of "Franking Officer.")		

TO: ~~IV Devis~~ ~~5 Glosters~~ ~~184 MGC~~ 184 (?) TMB
~~CH Group~~

| Sender's Number. | Day of Month. | In reply to Number. | A A A |
| G 210 | 15. | | |

Reference G.202 para 1 (1) line
5 for N.13.d.8/2.5 read N.13.d.1/2.5.
aaa acknowledge.

(4)

Acknowledged
15/5/16

From 184 Inf Bde
Place
Time 2.40 pm.

The above may be forwarded as now corrected. (Z)

Re App Traps

SECRET

4 Oxfords.	182 Inf Bde.
1 R.Berks.	2 Field Coy.
5 Glosters.	3 Field Coy.
2 Bucks.	M.T.M.B.
184 Machine Gun Coy.	"A" Coy Pioneers.
184 L.T.M.B.	3 Aust Tunnelling Coy.
Bde Signal Officer.	61 Div.
Left Group R.F.A.	War Diary.
15 Aust Bde.	

Programme for night 15/16 August 1916

1. The following programme will be carried out tonight 15/16 August.

   (i) 0.00 – 0.10   Artillery, Medium Trench Mortars, Light Trench Mortars, and Rifle Grenades to concentrate on enemy's front parapet from N.13.c.8½.1. to N.13.d.1½.5. Vickers Guns searching the ground in front of enemy's parapet.

   N.13.d.1½.5 = N.13.d.1½.5

   (ii) 0.10 – 0.15   Artillery lift to 2nd Line. Machine Guns on parapet.

   (iii) 0.15 – 0.20   Medium and Light Trench Mortars on Parapet. Artillery to remain on 2nd Line.

   (iv) 0.20 – 0.30   Machine Guns on 2nd Line – Mortars on Wire – Guns on back area.

   (v) 0.30 – 0.40   Guns back on to Parapet.

2. Particular attention to be paid to enemy mine shafts.

3. One day's ammunition.

4. Zero time 10.0 p.m.

5. Watches will be synchronised by Brigade Signal Officer at 6 p.m. by code.

Acknowledge

August 15th 1916.

G.H.Simpson Hayward
Capt.
for Major,
Brigade Major.
184th Infantry Brigade.

Acknowledged 15/8/16

"A" Form.
Army Form C. 2121.

MESSAGES AND SIGNALS.

No. of Message: ....

Prefix .... Code .... m. Words Charge

Office of Origin and Service Instructions.

SECRET.

This message is on a/c of:

.... Service.

Sent At .... m.
To ....
By ....

(Signature of "Franking Officer.")

Recd. at .... m.
Date ....
From ....
By ....

TO { H.Q. Bde.   5 Gloster.   184 M.G.C.   J.B. [Smb]
     Left Group

Sender's Number.	Day of Month.	In reply to Number.	
G.220.	16.		A A A

Reference G 217. aaa in each operation the MGs will start firing 10 minutes before the time hour.

From 184 Inf Bde.
Place
Time 2.10 pm.

The above may be forwarded as now corrected. (Z)

Censor. Signature of Addressor or person authorised to telegraph in his name.

* This line should be erased if not required.

SECRET.

4 Oxfords.	15 Aust Bde.
4 Royal Berks.	182 Inf Bde.
5 Glosters.	2 Field Coy.
2 Bucks Bn.	3 Field Coy.
184 M.G.C.	A Coy 5 Cornwalls.
184 L.T.M.B.	3 Aust Tunnelling Coy.
Bde Signal Officer.	61 Div.
Left Group R.F.A.	

1. The following programme will be carried out tonight 16/17 August

Operation A

(i)   0.00 - 0.10   Artillery, M.T.M's, L.T.M's, and Rifle Grenades to concentrate on enemy's front line and wire from N.14.a.6.2½. to N.14.a.9½.7.

(ii) 0.10 - 0.15   Lift on to enemy 2nd Line and Communication trenches in rear of (i)

(iii) 0.11 - 0.15   Vickers and Lewis Guns to sweep enemy parapet.

(iv) 0.15 - 0.30   No firing.

Operation B.

(v)   0.30 - 0.40   Artillery, M.T.M's, L.T.M's, and Rifle Grenades to concentrate on enemy front line and wire from N.19.a.6½.9. to N.19.a.3½.4.

(vi) 0.40 - 0.45   Lift on to enemy 2nd Line and Communication trenches in rear of (v).

(vii) 0.41 - 0.45   Vickers and Lewis Guns to sweep enemy parapet.

(viii) 0.45 - 1.00 No firing.

Operation C.

(ix) 1.00 - 1.10   Artillery and Rifle Grenades on enemy front line trench and wire from N.14.c.4.9. to N.13.d.9.6.   M.T.M's, and L.T.M's on enemy's wire at same point.

(x). 1.10 - 1.15   Lift on to enemy 2nd Line and communication trenches in rear of (ix).

(xi) 1.11 - 1.15   Vickers and Lewis Guns to sweep enemy parapet.

2. Particular attention to be paid to enemy mine shafts.

3. O.C. Machine Gun Coy will as well enfilade the German front line trenches as much as possible.

4. One days ammunition will be fired by M.T.M. and L.T.M's

5. Zero time will be 2.a.m.

6. Watches will synchronised by Bde Signal Officer at 7.45 p.m. on the telephone by code.

ACKNOWLEDGE.

August 16th 1916.

E C Gapp.
Major, Brigade Major
184th Infantry Brigade.

SECRET.
4/Oxfords.   15. Aust. Bde.
4/Royal Berks.   182 Inf. Bde.
5/Glosters.   2 Field Coy. R.E.
2/Bucks.   3 Field Coy. R.E.
184 M.G. Coy.   A Coy. 5/Cornwalls.
184 L.T.M.B.   3 Aust. Tunnelling Coy.
Bde Signal Officer. 61 Div.
Left Group, R.F.A.

The following Programme will be carried out to-night 17/18th August.

1. OPERATION "A".

   (i)   0.00. – 0.10.   M.T.M's on enemy's wire from N.8.d.5.2. – N.14.b.¼.8.

   (ii) 0.10. – 0.20.   Artillery, M.T.Ms. L.TMs to concentrate on enemy's front line and wire from N.8.d.5.2. – N.14.b.¼.8.

   (iii) 0.20. – 0.25.   Lift on to enemy's 2nd Line & C.Ts in rear of (i).

   (iv) 0.21. – 0.25.   Vickers and Lewis Guns to sweep enemy's parapet.

   (v)   0.25. – 0.40.   No firing.

2. OPERATION "B"

   (vi) 0.40. – 0.50.   M.TM's on enemy's wire from N.14.a.5¾.1. to N.14.c.2¼.7½.

   (vii) 0.50. – 1.00.   Artillery, M.T.Ms, L.T.Ms and rifle grenades to concentrate on enemy's front line and wire from N.14.a.5¾.1. to N.14.c.2¼.7½.

   (viii) 1.00. – 1.05. Lift on to enemy's 2nd line and C.Ts in rear of (vi)

   (ix) 1.00. – 1.05.   Vickers and Lewis Guns to sweep enemy's parapet.

   (x)   1.05. – 1.20.   No firing.

3. OPERATION. "C".

   (xi) 1.20. – 1.30.   Same as (i).
   (xii) 1.30. – 1.40.   "   " (ii).
   (xiii) 1.40. – 1.45.   "   " (iii)
   (xiv) 1.40. – 1.45.   "   " (iv)

4. In each case ^for the first 10 minutes the Artillery Fire will be Section Fire 15 secs.

5. Particular attention to be paid to enemy's mine shafts.

6. One day's ammunition will be fired by M.T.Ms and L.T.Ms.

7. Zero time will be 10-45 p.m.

8. Watches will be synchronised by Bde. Signal Officer at 6 p.m. by code on telephone.

ACKNOWLEDGE.

EC Gepp
Major
Brigade Major
184th Infantry Brigade.

B.H.Q.
August 17th, 1916.

4 Oxfords.
4 Royal Berks.
5 Glosters.
2 Bucks Bn.
184 M.G.C.
184 L.T.M.B.
Left Group R.F.A.

15 Aust Bde.
182 Inf Bde.
2 Fld Coy.
3 Fld Coy.
A Coy 5 Cornwalls.
3 Aust Tunnelling Coy.
61 Div.

Reference G.243 para 7 for 9.30 read 11.

ACKNOWLEDGE.

Major.
Brigade Major.
184 Inf Bde.

18.8.16.

SECRET

Oxfords.   15 Aust Bde
Royal Berks.   182 Inf Bde.
Glosters.   3 Field Coy R.E.
Bucks Bn.   2 Field Coy R.E.
34 M.G.C.   A Coy 5 Cornwalls.
34 L.T.M.B.   3 Aust Tunnelling Coy.
Bde Signal Officer: 61 Div.
1st Group R.F.A.

The following programme will be carried out tonight 18/19 August.

1. Operation A

   (i)   0.00 - 0.10   M.T.M's on enemy's wire from N.14.a.5¾.1.
                         to N.14.c.2¼.7½.

   (ii)   0.10 - 0.20   Artillery, M.T.Ms, L.T.Ms, and Rifle
                         Grenades to concentrate on enemy's front
                         line and wire from N.14.a.5¾.1. to
                         N.14.c.2¼.7½.

   (iii)   0.20 - 0.25   Lift on to enemy 2nd Line and C.T's in
                         rear of (i)

   (iv)   0.20 - 0.25   Vickers and Lewis Guns to sweep enemy
                         parapet.

   (v)   0.25 - 0.35   No firing.

   Operation B.

   (vi)   0.35 - 0.45   M.T.Ms on enemy wire from M.21.d.8.4¾.
                         to M.24.d.4.½.

   (vii)   0.45 - 0.55   Artillery, M.T.Ms, L.T.Ms, and Rifle Grenades
                         to concentrate on enemy front line and wire
                         from M.24.d.8.4¾. to M.24.d.4.½.

   (viii) 0.55 - 1.00   Lifts on to enemys 2nd Line and C.Ts in
                         rear of (vi)

   (ix)   0.55 - 1.00   Vickers and Lewis Guns to sweep enemy
                         parapet.

   (x)   1.00 - 1.30   No firing.

2. Operation C.

   (xi)   1.30 - 1.40   same as (i)
   (xii)   1.40 - 1.50   same as (ii)
   (xiii) 1.50 - 1.55   same as (iii)
   (xiv)   1.50 - 1.55   same as (iv)

4. In each operation, for the first seven minutes of Artillery fire, the Artillery will fire section fire 15 seconds, and for the last 3 minutes gun fire.

5. Particular attention to be paid to enemy mine shafts.

6. M.T.Ms will fire as fast as possible - L.T.Ms one days ammunition per mortar.

7. Zero time 9.30 p.m.

8. Watches will be synchronised by Bde Signal Officer at 5.30 p.m. on telephone by code.

Acknowledge

G.H. Simpson Hayward
Capt for
~~Major.~~
Bde Major.
183th Infantry Brigade

August 18th 1916.

SECRET   NOT TO BE TAKEN IN THE TRENCHES.

 Copy No. 10

184TH BRIGADE ORDER NO. 28

Reference
Trench Maps
1/10,000

August 17th 1916.

1. (a) Raiding Parties of the 5/GLOSTERS & 2/OXFORDS will carry out an enterprise against the enemy's lines between N.14.c.4.9. and N.14.c.2.7. on the 19/20th August.

   (b) The points of entry of the Raiding parties will be N.14.c.4.8½ and N.14.c.2¾.7¾.

   (c) The Raiding parties will capture and hold the square formed by the following points:- N.14.c.4.8½., along enemy's Communication Trench to his support line at N.14.c.5½.8., thence along his support line to N.14.c.4.6¾., thence back to his front line at N.14.c.2¾.7¾.

2. The object of the Raid is :-

   (a) To take prisoners.

   (b) Destroy emplacements.

   (c) To obtain identifications.

   (d) Destroy enemy's mine shafts in the vicinity- (a Party of No.3. Australian Tunnelling Coy. will be detailed to accompany Raiding Parties for this purpose).

3. Details of the Raid will be arranged between the Officers Commanding the Battalions concerned.

4. Lt.Colonel P. Balfour 5/GLOSTERS will issue the necessary detailed orders for the operation, and will be in Command of the Troops engaged in the enterprise. He will be known as O.C. Raid.

5. O.C. Left Group, R.F.A. will detail a Liaison Officer to report to O.C. Raid at his Advanced Headquarters and remain with him during the Operation.
This Officer will arrange to be connected up by wire with the Left Group Commander who will be with Advanced Brigade Headquarters near HOUGOUMONT (M.12.c.2.8.)

6. (a) The Artillery of the Left Group assisted by Heavy Medium and Light Trench Mortars will co-operate in accordance with Time Table "A" attached.

6. (b) On days prior to the date of the enterprise the Artillery and Trench Mortars will, in order to deceive the enemy, carry out wire-cutting at different points along the front as well as at that portion of the enemy's line selected for the Raiding Parties to enter. When firing at this last named point particular attention will be paid to the wire in front of the places where the Raiding parties will enter (para.1 b. above) Special instructions regarding this preliminary wire-cutting will be issued from day to day from Brigade Headquarters.

(c) In order to further deceive the enemy the Artillery and Mortars will, on the day of the enterprise (19th) before zero hour at times to be notified by Bde.H.Q. bombard enemy's line and wire.

   (i) at the places selected for Raiding parties to enter.

   (ii) At other parts of the enemy's line. (These parts will be notified to Artillery Commander from Bde.H.Qrs.)

After firing as detailed above in (c) (i) & (ii), Guns and Mortars will be laid ready to co-operate in the raid at Zero hour.

7. The 184th Machine Gun Company will, on the day of the Raid, fire in accordance with attached Time Table B. On days and hours prior to the date and hour of the Raid, the Brigade Machine Guns will :-

   (i) Prevent enemy repairing gaps in the wire.

   (ii) Co-operate with the Artillery as laid down in para. 6 (c.) (i) & (ii) above.

8. Action of Lewis Guns in Front Line.

   (i) Prior to Raid. Prevent enemy repairing gaps in wire.

   (ii) During Raid. Engage hostile Machine Guns and rifles in accordance with orders to be issued by O.C. Raid.

9. Signals from Liaison Officer with O.C. Raid to Left Group Commander (if wire is cut) :-

   (i) Guns to lengthen Range.)
   (ii) Guns to shorten Range.) Visual in accordance
   (iii) Guns to come back on enemy's parapet.) with special instructions from Group Commander.

10. Prisoners will be sent to TEMPLE BAR (WHITE HOUSE) M.12.c. Central)

~~11.   Watches will be synchronised on the 19th at 4 p.m. on the 19th inst~~

11.   Watches will be synchronised on the 19th inst at 4 p.m. and 8 p.m. by code on telephone by the Bde. Signal Officer.

12.   The following Traffic orders will be enforced during the Operation:-

    Orderlies, Runners etc :-

    UP or IN.   RIFLEMANS AV.

    DOWN or OUT. SUTHERLAND AV.

    Casualties to be evacuated via PICANTIN AV.

13.   Zero time will be issued later.

14.   Advanced Brigade Headquarters will be established at HOUGOUMONT (M.12.c.2.8.) one hour before zero.

15.   Reports to Advanced Brigade Headquarters.

<u>ACKNOWLEDGE</u>

                          E.C. Gepp
                               Major
                          Brigade Major
                     184th Infantry Brigade.

Issued at :- 10 a.m.

Copy No. 1. to 4. Bde. Staff.
            5. 4/Oxfords.
            6. 4/R.Berks.
            7. 5/Glosters.
            8. 2/Bucks.
            9. 184th Machine Gun Coy.
          10. 184th Light Trench Mortars.
          11. 61st Div.
          12. 182 Infantry Brigade.
          13. 15th Australian Bde.
          14. 3rd Australian Tunnelling Co.
          15. Left Group. R.F.A.

SECRET

4/Oxfords
5/Glosters.
4/Royal Berks.
184 Machine Gun Coy.
15 Aust Bde.
182 Inf. Bde.

184 L.T.M.B.
Left Group, R.F.A.
3 Aust. Tunnelling Co.
2 Bucks Bn.
61 Div.

---

1. Reference 184 Infantry Brigade Order No.26 dated 17/8/16.

2. Zero time will be 10.40 p.m.

3. An amended Time Table "A" is issued herewith. Previous copy will be destroyed.

ACKNOWLEDGE.

E.C. Gepp, Major
Brigade Major
184th Infantry Brigade.

B.H.Q.
19/8/16.

	TIME.		Guns.	Objective.	Rate of Fire.	Remarks.
	From	To.				
7.	0.00.	0.02.	2 L.T.Ms.	Front Line and wire N.14.c.5.7½ to N.14.c.4½.8¼.	Rapid.	
8.	0.00.	0.05.	1 L.T.M.	On point N.14.a.6½.2½.	Rapid.	
9.	0.00.	1.15"	H.T.M.	On N. & E. of WICK.	"	
10.	0.10"	0.15"	On 18 Pounders	Lift 100 yards.	Section fire 30 secs.	
11.	0.03.	1.15, or until signal to stop.	2 M.T.Ms.	On M.G.E. at N.13.d.9.6. and N.14.a.7½.4.	As quickly as possible.	
12.	0.02.	0.05.	2 L.T.Ms.	SUPPORT LINE N.14.c.4¾.6½ to N.14.c.4½.8½.	1 Round per 5 secs.	
13.	0.03.	Until further orders.	1 L.T.M.	N.14.c.4.6. to N.14.c.7½. 6½.	5 Rounds per minute.	
14.	0.05.	Until further orders.	3 L.T.M.	At point N.14.a.6½.2½.	6 Rounds per minute.	
15.	0.15.	1.15 or until signal given to stop.	18 Pounders.	Forming barrage round occupied Trench	Section fire 15 secs.	

ZERO HOUR .... AMENDED TIME TABLE "A" ISSUED WITH 184TH INFANTRY BRIGADE ORDER NO.28.

	TIME		Guns.	Objective.	Rate of Fire	Remarks.
	From	To				
1.	10 min before zero.	Zero.	2 M.T.Ms.	Wire at point of entry	As quickly as possible.	
2.	Zero. Infantry will advance towards objective as far as our Artillery & Mortar fire will permit.					
	0.00.	0.10.	18 Pounders.	Front Line N.13.d.8½.6½. - N.14.a.6½.2½.	Section fire 10 secs.	
3.	0.00.	1.15 or until signal given to stop.	4.5"	At points N.13.d.9.6¼ and N.14.a.6½.2½.	Section fire 30 secs.	
4.	0.00.	1.15 or until signal given to stop.	4.5"	At points N.14.c.2.4. and b. 14.a. 8¼.1¼.	Section fire One minute.	
5.	0.00.	1.15.	6"	On WICK.		
6.	0.00.	0.05.	2 M.T.Ms.	On parapet at point of entry.	As quickly as possible.	

P.T.O.

SECRET

4/Oxfords	184th Machine Gun Coy.	1/5 Cornwalls.
4/Royal Berks	184th Light Trench Mortars.	182 Inf. Bde.
5/Glosters	2 Field Coy. R.E.	61 Div.
2/Bucks.	3 Field Coy. R.E.	3 Australian Tunnelling Coy.

Artillery, M.T.M. L.T.M. & M.G. Programme for August 23rd.

1. Object to worry enemy in his consolidation of Crater at M.24.d.2½.1. To destroy enemy's mineshafts at M.30.b.3¾.9¾.
   NOTE:- Exact position of Mineshaft can be seen at Bde. Headquarters.

   Object

2. (i)   0.00. -0.08   2 M.T.Ms. on Crater.

   (ii) 0.02. -0.05   Artillery on Crater.

   (iii) 0.00. -0.05   1 L.T.M. on Crater rapid fire.

   (iv) 0.05. -0.20   Artillery on enemy's front line from M.30.b.2.8. to M.24.d.5¾.2¼.

   (v)   0.07. -0.10   1 L.T.M. on enemy's C.T. at M.30.b.5.9½.   To catch enemy withdrawing from Front line.

   (vi) 0.08. -0.20   2 M.T.Ms. on Mineshaft.

   (vii) 0.10. -0.15   1 L.T.M. on enemy's front line from M.30.b.1½.7½. to M.30.b.2.8.   To catch enemy moving to a flank.

   (viii) 0.10. -0.15 1 L.T.M. on enemy's front line from M.24.d.6.2. to M.24.d.6.3¼.   Ditto.

   (ix). 0.20. -0.25   Artillery lift to enemy's support line in rear of (iv)

   (x). 0.22. -0.25   Vickers and Lewis Guns sweep enemy's front parapet.   To catch heads.

3. Zero time 9-30 p.m.

   ACKNOWLEDGE.

W. Dugan Brig.Genl.

Major
Brigade Major
184th Infantry Brigade.

B.H.Q. 22/8/16.